CLEAVE

CLEAVE

tiana nobile

poems

HUB CITY PRESS
SPARTANBURG, SC

Book design: Kate McMullen
Cover Painting © Eden Some
Editor: Leslie Sainz
Proofreader: Amanda Linnette Rosa, Kendall Owens
Author Photo: Zoe Cuneo

Text: Arno Pro 10.5 / 14
Display: Sommet Slab Regular

Library of Congress Cataloging-in-Publication Data

Names: Nobile, Tiana, author.
Title: Cleave : poems / Tiana Nobile.
Description: Spartanburg, SC : Hub City Press, 2021.
Summary: "In her debut collection, Tiana Nobile grapples with the history of transnational adoption, both her own from South Korea and the broader, collective experience. In conversation with psychologist Harry Harlow's monkey experiments and utilizing fragments of a highly personal cache of documents from her own adoption, these poems explore dislocation, familial relationships, and the science of love and attachment."
Identifiers: LCCN 2020047490
ISBN 9781938235757 (paperback)
ISBN 9781938235764 (ebook)
Subjects: LCGFT: Poetry.
Classification: LCC PS3614.O23 C58 2021
DDC 813/.6--dc23
LC record available at https://lccn.loc.gov/2020047490

Hub City Press gratefully acknowledges support from the National Endowment for the Arts, the Amazon Literary Partnership, South Arts, and the South Carolina Arts Commission.

HUB CITY PRESS
200 Ezell Street
Spartanburg, SC 29306
1.864.577.9349

TABLE OF CONTENTS

III.

My mother groand! my father wept.
Into the dangerous world I leapt:
Helpless, naked, piping loud;
Like a fiend hid in a cloud.

–*William Blake, "Infant Sorrow"*

I.

MOON YEONG SHIN

Written on the white slip at the bottom
of a polaroid, cut off by the frame:
a name. Many years passed before I learned
surnames come first in Korea. I rode
my bicycle in circles around this reversal.
For years, my skin leaped from shadow to shadow.
I drank the darkness, or the darkness drank me,
but what's the difference when your veins are full
of haunting? One day I will walk
the narrow streets of many cities full of ice
freshly frozen. I will hike through forests
of wind storms newly risen. I will learn
and forget the names of many trees,
of tea leaves plucked too early in the season.
I will orbit the earth like a moon
searching for its shadow. Where does a moon
find its planet? Or is it the other way
around? To be a recently hatched egg-moon,
curved shell pinned to the sky. I've spent my whole
life in orbit of other people's light, celestial satellite
in ceaseless wane. How much can you learn
from a stranger's surname? A young animal
crawls its way out of the womb, stretches its legs,
and feels cold for the very first time.

/ˈmaᴛʜəʀ/

We tend to our roles like we tend to a fire,
    poking the coals with the blazing tip of an iron.

The head of a woman occasionally produces more heads.
    The body of a woman is the source of all our breaths.

See Also: The naming of riverbanks.
    See Also: Nature's tendency to cleave.

There is a difference between the qualities
    we inherit and the qualities of instinct.

The brain with its many folds looks like it's squeezing itself.
    Its mouths are puckered and waiting to be unlocked with a kiss.

An organ of the body is regarded as the source
    of nourishment for the next corresponding organ.

How we feed on each other for ourselves.
    How we keep ourselves alive through each other.

You are the living tissue beneath the bark of a cork oak.
    You are a ship grained with the grooves of trees.

WHAT ORCHARD ARE YOU FROM?

The juice of the berry, of black, of blue,
of red. You sweep the sweet dripping
off your chin with your tongue. In the folds
of your cheeks, you savor the sap.

Who is to say they know the
power of fruit?
That which could not be
picked?

They call me peach,
orange soft and tender peel.
They bundle my bones in boxes
and ship them across continents
to be packaged and sold.

Who is to say they weren't
made to poison?

Left out on the counter, my flesh will darken.
Taste the bitter pulp, the slender tendon
where the stem snapped.

What will rot where the skin
was bit?

Take me by the jowl,
the stony pit
I keep buried in my mouth.

Do you still feel where they
snipped the stalk?

Even my most succulent fruit
will never fully ripen.
Pruned premature, I ache for root.

ABSTRACT

"The surrogate was made from a block of wood, covered with sponge rubber, and sheathed in tan cotton terry cloth. A light bulb behind her radiated heat. The result was a mother, soft, warm, and tender, a mother with infinite patience, a mother available twenty-four hours a day, a mother that never scolded her infant and never struck or bit her baby in anger. . . ."

–Harry Harlow, "The Nature of Love"

Mother of Ghost

Whether of wire or terrycloth,
there will always be
Mother. Mine was made
of ghost. Every move is
one step away from her.
I try to backtrack, lose myself in maps.
I tell myself, *Tread nimbly.*
Every step is a newborn
shadow. Bodies
fracturing light.

MOTHER OF LETTERS

For hours my mother hovered over us,
her hand gently guiding mine, her wrist
a helm for my unsteady ship.
I knew how to hold a pencil,
how to grip it between my thumb
and pointer finger, how to lean softly
to avoid a callus. I knew how to form
all my letters perfectly before starting school.
For every birthday, a new notebook
would appear wrapped tightly with a bow.
I would bury my nose inside it
as if the pages would write themselves
with my breath. The pages I'd fill with words
my young tongue was too knotted to express.

ST. ROSE OF LIMA

Lips weary with chapped hallelujahs,
you went to church and learned the power
of patience. You used to sit in the pew

and wonder how long it would take before your tears
would turn to blood, how many prayers
you must memorize to be worthy

of that kind of miracle.
Stained glass windows glowed
multicolored portraits of a woman

in prayer. Rose was your patron saint.
While writing this poem you discover
she's the protector of florists,

embroiderers, and "people ridiculed
or misunderstood for their piety."
Your brother's laughter rings out

from across the kitchen table
all these years later. No one ever asked
why your hair was falling out.

While you pretended not to notice
the bald spot on your scalp, you collected
the strands of hair and fashioned them

into crosses. In school you learned Lima
is a city in South America,
but all you could think about was her forehead

wrapped with spikes, her waist weighed down
by an iron chain. She made her bed with broken glass
and stone. The thought of her locking the door

and burning her hands burned like a looping film
on the inside of your eyelids.
You knelt at the cross and kept your hands

in your pockets, pricking your thumb against
the thorn you found in the garden.
For years, you slept on the floor

of your little sister's bedroom,
afraid to talk to the darkness alone.
You asked god for a new

mattress. Nightmares shattered you
like mirrors. You turned the lights off
and on and off and on and off and on.

Isn't this the cost of being alive?
You challenge yourself.
You rock yourself to sleep.

THE NIGHT I DREAMED OF WATER

A man in a boat scoops water
one rounded palm at a time.
His hands are porous. He sticks the tip
of his tongue out of the corner of his mouth
like a turtle. The water rises. It is my father.
He is carrying my elderly aunt across
his shoulders like a yoke.
She is wailing. Her hair is stormy,
but her clothes are matching.
We are in her 93rd Street apartment.
I can smell her skin on the pillowcases.
Flowers are wilting off the wallpaper.
Her silk scarf whirls in the wind. I collect
the parched petals. Curve my hand
like the bent bottom of a boat. Petals leak
through my fingers. The water continues to rise.
There is no boat, just a man
scooping water with his hands.
Front to back. Side to side.

Intercourse, *Pennsylvania*. Fertile, *Iowa*. Uncertain, *Texas*. Hazard, *Nebraska*. Accident, *Maryland*. Why, *Arizona*. Hell, *Michigan*. Disappointment, *Kentucky*. Embarrass, *Minnesota*. Truth Or Consequences, *New Mexico*. Nameless, *Tennessee*. No Name, *Colorado*. Nada, *Texas*. Nothing, *Arizona*.

ABSTRACT

Mother Without a Face

looks in the mirror. I wonder what creases we share. I wonder how long her hair is. I wonder if she chews on the inside of her mouth until the skin is chafed pulp, if she sucks her teeth when it rains. I wonder if she clings to heat like a monkey to cloth.

My nose capsizes, an upside down question mark. I pull and pull, the line stretched short.

MOTHER OF ROCK

The familiar *clack* of shoes against tile, *click*
of the key in the lock. Wait and rock.

Your gaze silent and grim, I long for the touch
that doesn't come. My tongue caught

on my mouth's cage
tart with sour milk.

In the picture from your wedding,
a white lace dress. As if held

down by the weight of fancy fabric,
your bones ache to float off the edges

of the frame. Mother of stone,
teach me the temperature

of tomb. Watch me chase my tail.
Toss me a cloth, a bottle of milk.

my sister was Fed-Exed from Korea?
you say, dazed under the haze of hospital lights,
your arm tethered to an intravenous drip
charging like a box to numbing light.
You're twenty-five, adrift in anesthetic fog
floating through the white sea of hospital hallways,
and you think of me, the living package
that changed your life. On the day of my arrival,
you were a month away from turning four.
While the buzz of anticipation swirled
around the airport terminal, your small body
perched high, anchored in the crook of our father's arm.
So this is how babies are born,
you thought, and everything was yellow.
Scuffed linoleum tile. Blur of fluorescent lights
hovering above you. How you must have imagined
my body rattling in the box during transport
as our mother scurried to the airport bathroom
to snap my joints into place.
Today, we laugh about what you said.
We laugh until we forget why we're laughing.

ABSTRACT

Foster Mother

The first time I belonged to a woman,
my body a fresh bulb broken off

at the root. She kept me for six months,
watched spit bubble from my pursed lips.

I wonder if she ever claimed me,
if she rocked me to sleep on her chest,

if she wiped my mouth gently saying,
There you go, there you are.

MOTHER OF CLOTH

During hurricanes, my body tucked tightly
under blankets and eyes illuminated
by the pale luster of a plastic nightlight,

you drew curly cues along my spine
with your index finger, patted my back
to the beat of rain pounding on the window.

When there's a storm, it means they're bowling in heaven.

Claps of thunder are balls tossed
down the lane. Each flash of lightning
means an angel just got a strike.

We would count the seconds between thunder –
one mississippi, two mississippi, three . . .
and I'd shudder in my sheets, hands clasped in prayer
begging god to hurry up and end the party.

You wrapped my body in cloth,
held my hand until you felt the fingers
loosen and fall. The next time I woke,

I called your name. And you would come.
You always came.

Dreams of Motherhood

Wire barbed with fragments of love
or tender cloth that never scolds,
never strikes, never bites?

The mothers I find like copper coins,
heads face up. The ones I collect
because of their tenderness.
The nature of a light radiating heat.

Monkey in the cage, pulling out her hair,
waiting for someone to claim her.
What is the opposite of mother?

CHILD'S PRE-FLIGHT REPORT

Name in Full: Moon, Yeong Shin
Date of Birth: Oct. 22, 1987
Name of Escort: Unknown

Case Number: 87C-2411
Date of Departure: April 2, 1988
Destination: Unknown

Feeding/Eating: She cries with hunger but knows the bottle.

Sleeping Habit: When lying on her side, she wraps her arms around her body. She wakes easily to rustling leaves, rain thrumming on roof tiles, and morning birds greeting the dawn.

Toilet Training: She moves bowels in good form once to twice a day.

Speaking Ability: She will learn quickly when to bite her tongue. For years, she will hold it tightly, teeth clenched. In her mouth, the bitter taste of a broken bloodline.

Developmental Condition: She tends to play well even alone but cries if it's boring. Placed on stomach, she lifts her head about 90 degrees but gets irritated when it's beyond her ability.

Physical Condition: 6.6 kg., 60 cm at 5 months. Her skin is strong but prone to scarring.

Character: She is rather composed and mild.

Legal Status:

The baby, … if it is to survive, must clutch at more than a straw.

–*Harry Harlow, "The Nature of Love"*

II.

/ˈmɪɡrənt/

Of an animal, especially a bird. A wandering species
whom no seas nor places limit. A seed who survives despite
the depths of hard winter. The ripple of a herring

steering her band from icy seas to warmer strands.
To find the usual watering-places despite
the gauze of death that shrouds our eyes

is a breathtaking feat. Do you ever wonder why
we felt like happy birds brushing our feathers
on the tips of leaves? How we lifted our toes

from one sandbank and landed – fingertips first –
on another? Why we clutched the dumb and tiny creatures
of flower and blade and sod between our budding fists?

From an origin of buried seeds emerge
these many-banded dagger wings.
We, of the sky, the dirt, and the sea. We,

the seven-league-booters and the little-by-littlers.
We, transmigrated souls, will prevail.
We will carry ourselves into the realms of light.

THE STOLEN GENERATION

i. The Severing

To pull apart, separated by skin and stock
To set asunder, taken and scattered like dandelion seeds
To part or open (the lips, eyelids), examine with a fine-tooth comb
To slice the skull and measure the brain, to prove what is already
    known
To cleave a family and watch it unravel
To hinder reunification
To disjoin a body from its color
To disperse its history, its memory, its own recognition of self
To make sense of a loss that severe

ii. The Snatching

1869 11th November

BE IT ENACTED. . .

It shall be lawful

        from time to time

                to make orders

to rescind

      or alter

           that is to say

For the place of –

      For the care custody and education of –

From time to time

Every child living

      shall be deemed to be within,

            under, before justice.

                1886 2nd September

WHEREAS. . .

The duty to care

      The duty to care

           to protect

iii. The Searching

To make sense of a loss that severe
they searched for each other
for one hundred years.

One mother would hide
her daughter in plain sight
by blanketing her body

with charcoal. They didn't take
full-bloods, only the ones
with hints of European blush

in their cheeks.
One day they went to the river
and forgot the power of water.

Charcoal carried off the body
in a rippling sweep.
They carried her away, skin still gray-wet.

Another mother brought her infant son
to the hospital sick with a stomach bug.
She left him for treatment

and six months later implored,
I am writing to ask if you would let me know
how B– is and how long before

I can have him back home.
I have not forgot
I got a baby in there.

iv. The Cleaving

The word "cleave" means both to cut and to cling.
The child cleaved to her mother   The child cleaved from her mother
The difference a word makes in the forest of our longing.

He cleaved to the bed, body damp with dream sweat, eyes sealed so tightly
rivulets of tears streamed from the corners. His mind cleaved
to the fading image of a woman's (a mother's?) tender face.

Body buoyant and brown, she was cloven from the river.
Mid-stroke, her limbs cleaved like the frayed ends of a rope.

How do you begin to reconcile a cleaving?
We try to hold each other   without touching
Voices scramble   white noise fills our bones

THE LAST STRAW

"U.S. woman put adopted Russian son on one-way flight alone back to
homeland"

–NY Post headline, 9 April 2010

Little boy in a yellow jacket

stinger pinned   to the   zipper

  on his   chest   a note

    written in a hand

not his   own   Russia-bound

     After giving my best. . . for the safety of. . .

Who   belongs   to whom?

  How   do we   dance   without

  the proper   shoes?

     He drew a picture. . .

The carousel

  of   abandonment

      endlessly

    spinning

     Of our house burning. . .

How many

    splinters

does it take

        to start

            a fire?

     I was lied to . . . misled by . . .

A fuse

        a body

   pleas for

        water

nothing

        but

        matches

OPERATION BABYLIFT

"We bucket-brigade-loaded the children right up the stairs into the
airplane."

–Col. Bud Traynor, pilot

April 4, 1975

Skin still wet with mother's grief.
I brought my baby to them,
I admit it.

Airlift Takes Off

Tucked in cardboard and stowed.
Two to each seat.

At 23,000 Feet Systems Fail

In the event of being born
in a country ravaged by war –

Explosion

I heard rumors that mixed babies
would be burned alive. Retaliation
for consorting with the enemy.

Split Cables

Save – Rescue – Liberate

Descends

I asked about the papers. How
will I find her? How will we reunite
in America?

Skids in Rice Paddy

       In the event their skin is soaked in gasoline –

4:45pm

            Those who didn't fit
            would make the trip
             in the cargo area.

Crosses Saigon River

          Under the circumstances,
       the evacuation became necessary –

Thrashes Trench

           The promise of reunion
           too appealing to pass up.

Fractures in Four

      Jam-packed flock, throng of new bones.

Fuel Ignites

          It was no longer a choice.

Fifty Adults

            The only option.

& Seventy-Eight Children

FIRE AND RICE

"There were large sheaves of papers and batches of babies. Who knew
which belonged to which?"

*–Bobby Nofflet, worker with the U.S. Agency
for International Development in Saigon*

Though the first flight crashed,
it didn't stop them.

Planes full of moonless hair
black as peppercorn.

The mission seemed simple.
The same planes that shelled cities

swapped blitz for babies.
Procedural paperwork waived

to expedite departure.
Mothers made promises of *meet again* –

Yellow-haired surrogates burying
the truth of it –

Meet: In the dike next to the river,
mouths full of fire and rice.

What then may I do
but cleave to what cleaves me.

–Li-Young Lee, "The Cleaving"

III.

ABSTRACT

Igneous rocks are formed by fire. Conceived in the belly of a volcano, lava drips down its side and deposits at the base. As a result of cooler temperatures, the magma grows viscous on the earth's surface and undergoes a process of solidification. Basalt, granite, obsidian. Broken down by weathering and erosion, the rock will become sediment, loose bits of matter, the dregs. Later, these same pieces will accumulate and lithify to form sedimentary rocks. Conglomerate, limestone, sandstone. Over time, this same rock will succumb to pressure and sink back down inside the earth to be heated and melted, metamorphosized. Gneiss, marble, quartzite. Once deep enough in the earth's mantle, the metamorphic rock will liquefy and return to the magma chamber.

Or will the rock evade erosion, unwilling to be weathered? Will the rock rise up again instead of returning to its magma pillow? Or will the rock crumble into tiny particles of sand and pass its time in a shoal on the bottom of the ocean?

My body, a stone. Weathered, compacted, compressed. Softened by another body's tender heat. A hardened face wont to wince. If I jump from a cliff, will the canyon catch me? Or will I tumble, endlessly moving, endlessly seeking a place to rest my head?

What do   you taste   in the morning   when you   lick   your lips?
Are they soft   or split,   cracked   by the Wisconsin wind?   Do you
cover your mouth   when you   cough?   With your elbow or   your
hand?   When the germs   are floating   through   the air,   do you
imagine where they land?   How those minuscule microbes   descend
with invisible   parachutes?   The power of gravity   on weightless
spit?   Do you smirk   when they fall   in your   colleague's coffee?
How do you make sense   out of loneliness?   At night   beneath the
buzz of fluorescent light,   do you   unlatch the lock?   Do you count
their inhalations   as they sleep?   Do you taste   their morning breath?
The little bacteria   floating   in the air   and landing   on the tip of
your tongue?   If it lands on your   tongue,   do you swallow it?
Can you   tell me   what it tastes like?   Do you feel   the microbes
twist   as they sink   down your   esophagus?   How does it feel
to watch   them   hold   each other's   hands,   their woolly
knuckles   braided,   the touch of their   palms?   What
do you   do   when the lock   has been left open?
What do you do   when they   reach   through
the cage?   What do   you   do   when
they   stare   at   you   straight   in
your eyes   and   cough
in your open
mouth?

ABSTRACT

For the first six months, I was a deferred plane ticket.

Contact comfort is a variable of overwhelming importance

The infant the pastor refused to baptize.

The development of affectional responses

I never sucked my thumb. I pulled out my hair instead.

Emotionality indices such as vocalization, crouching,
rocking, and sucking

Call me Rhesus, macaque with mongolian spots.

We can be certain that

I cry with hunger but know the bottle.

Frantic clutching of their bodies was very common

MOTHER OF WOOD

When did you become a house? Hands budding
into ivory doorknobs, your mouth sewn
into the stitching of the couch. One night
I awoke to your fingers slipping needles
in my mouth. My tongue a tangled tapestry
you tried to mend. I never knew you
were such a good seamstress. You hung my body
from the shelf like one of those hard-cheeked dolls
with eyes that blink when you shake them.
When you watched your own mother sweep
stifled suffering under the carpet, did you know
you would raise a home built on the same fears?
On winter nights the house howls, and I wonder
if in sleep your mouth is open, ready to wail.

ABSTRACT

Because my body is a body,
I learn to yield. I collect lemons
from my lemon tree. I bury fish heads
in the garden. I remember the silence
of my childhood. The writing heat rising
from the grill. The roosters in my backyard
know nothing about dawn.
They crow all night long.

TO WHOM IT MAY CONCERN:

This letter is to verify that █████████████████████
has been placed in the home of Mr. and Mrs. ████████████
for the purpose of adoption.

████████ has not previously been baptized and we, ████████
██████████████████████ authorize Mr. and Mrs. ████████
to baptize their daughter .

Sincerely,

████████████

> Because infants cannot consent
> to baptism or transport, the pastor's concerns
> seemed reasonable.

THE CONDITIONS | *That the religious faith of said minor child is* unknown

THE REVIEW | *That the religious faith of the parents of said child is/are informed and verily believe* unknown

THE NAMING | *That the religious faith of petitioners is/are* Roman Catholic

THE CONSENT | *That said minor child has no property or means of support, except that* being provided by petitioners

THE RELEASE | *That on information and belief said minor child has* no *general or testamentary guardian*

THE ACQUISITION | *That said* ████████████ *shall henceforth be regarded and treated in all respects as the child of your petitioners*

THE CHRISTENING | *And be known and called by the name of* ████████████████

/ MUN /

Considering how changes influence the earth
is it impossible to reach a newly formed day?

Imagine the light of a new translucency,
new as a natural planet extending beyond its circuitry.

To be a crescent-shaped ornament
dangling from midnight's velvet coat,

to be a globe-shaped gaslight transmitting
somebody else's shine,

to be white as the porcelain base
of a fingernail.

The period of imprisonment in any one night
silvers into the sleeping one's hair.

An aperture at the center of a clock draws
its hands and says,

Sometimes lesser splendor reflects fits of frenzy.

Take this moon-eyed bottle of shine –
remember who owns the night.

THE COURIER

You will settle into your seat
and slacken your jaw. Before long,
your ears will pop as you cradle
your package, holding it

carefully like a Christmas ornament.
You will unwrap her like a tamale,
still warm and steaming.
The lighting on airplanes is never bright enough,

and the cold artificial air will arrive in bursts,
numbing your fingers as they clutch her
oh so tenderly. You will cover her in cloth.
Bind her in layers of pastel pajamas

until all that remains is a bulb-shaped face
encased in a pale blue blanket. Sunrise
will leak through the window,
yellow and low like a lion's morning growl.

You will touch her face.
She will never open her eyes.

MOTHER OF WIRE

If I had a choice . . .

mother of wire   barbed   and   wombless   my mouth poised   to pucker.

I tried my best given the tools I had, you say.   Where   were   you

while   I   crouched   in the   corner,

a nest   of shadows?

Bring out the hammer,   mother.

The statue of the virgin Mary   illuminates   my nightstand.

I   touch-touch-touch   kiss   her   foot

soaked   in snake's blood   splattered spots   of red acrylic.

In the dictionary   of childhood   illnesses

I seek   symptoms   that fit my   unraveling

hair   falling   in clumps   on the couch

tiny meticulous hands   counting   each   strand.

Call me Rhesus,

Young   and   Moonless,

monkey without a cloth

to dust her bones.

'LOST' FIRST LANGUAGES LEAVE PERMANENT MARK ON THE BRAIN, NEW STUDY REVEALS

To experience the world muffled
through the wall of skin
is like wearing earmuffs
while deep sea diving.
Cacophony of whalesong
and sunken earthquakes,
tonal pitches seep in.

     •

How do I translate
the sound of my mother's
moaning? It's a soft wail
I hang on the wall
of my windpipe.

     •

They say the circulatory system
is the first to develop
in an embryo.

That the body generates cells
to divide and multiply, to form
a swelling ball.

That your blood weaved and whirled
to become my blood.

Who was the first you told?

     •

At week eleven, fingernails begin to appear.
I bet you didn't know that nails
are made of dead blood cells.
How something could grow inside you
that's both alive and dead.

·

Once I learned how to talk, I did not
stop. I drew blood and licked my teeth
with language, English spilling down my chin.
Later, I learned how words can wound
without touching, and I tucked myself
in a bed of silence.

PETALS

My mind is a clenched cocoon
A fist of grindstone petals

I was a dancer before I was born
My dreams spun on the loom, stuck in its pedal

If I miss a step, snap and pirouette down the staircase
My feet will wrestle with the vines and the petals

I wish I knew time's seamstress
Eyelashes descend in petals

The past is a shoelace
Caught on bicycle chains and pedals

I ran along the railroad looking for you
My mouth stale with wine and burnt petals

In the morning, you, Moon, will be someone else
Daughter of a million buried petals

FATHER, HARRY (HOLY MAKER)

forgets his voice

alone in the office   torpid hum   fluorescent light

the science of love   intent on ruin

when he lost his second wife to cancer

they laid him on the table

father rhesus   electrode temples

brain full   of static   body   convulsing

his love   &   its meditations

father   of wire   of cloth   of macaque

sits at his desk

rocks   back   and   forth

reaches

tremors   in his hands

clutching   at   more   than   a   straw

UNDERWATER FALSETTO

for Muriel

How many tongues does it take to slice a heart?
Your mouth spills over your mouth.

A cage breaks apart. I watch
as you hold a moon
in your lips and feel the wind

of a wing take off from your tongue.
You paint yourself with blood
and wrap the night

around your shoulders. Or is the night
cradling you in its leather purse?

Some say to close your eyes. I say look
the ocean straight in its blue
and bulging face.

Water will flood through all your fissures.

You carry a heart in your pocket.
You wonder how long before it breaks.

/ˈmʌŋkɪ/

Does an animal belong to its tail,
or does a tail belong to its animal?

In what trees do they live?
In countries old or new?
What worlds do they hold
tucked in their cheek-pouches?

I have a flat nose, a sideways face.
Where the new world meets the old,
my nostrils point downward,
summon the breath of
capuchin, howler, moustache, proboscis,
rhesus, squirrel, spider, vervet.

We dress ourselves in furs.
Images of our likeness are carved into tree bark
with paws over our mouths,
paws over our eyes,
paws over our ears.

A foggy image begins to form in my third eye:
an organ-grinder cranks a barrel
with giant wooly hands.

It is late.
What is broken finds its way back to itself.
Like a soldering flux, we cleave.

Years later, I will tell you I remember the town made of wood, quilted houses with slanted rooftops. I will tell you I remember the hospital, the room where I curled like a bloodless earthworm looking for dirt, the smell of morning nesting in the window, night falling purple on the floor. You will believe me and be jealous. I will cling to this envy, covet it, keep it in a locket that hangs around my neck. I will tell you these things even if they aren't true. I will convince myself late into the night until I feel the grass grazing my toes, the sun's heat on my back.

HARLOW'S MONKEY

We learned to give ourselves away
early on. We used to hide the bruises,
used to scratch our arms until they bled,
until our body was a weeping wound.

The cage exists only in our mind.
Kick down the door. Matchstick.

Whether of wire or terrycloth, we all burn
the same. We gasp for air and taste the bitter juice
of roses, petals dried and clipped
to the pages of our chest.

At the feet of our gods, we pile our bones,
muscles threaded to flesh. The fresh liquor
of unchained thought burning the roof of our mouths,
we take back our tongues, drink handfuls of water.

In what shallow grave will we bury the words
we killed? *Eomeoni. Abeoji. Daejeon.*
Moon Yeong Shin. We deliver them
to the dirtmother and her family of worms.

The past mushrooms and burns
in atomic flush. We sling a new sun
from the pit of our stomachs
and raise our wooly hands, fingers clenched.

The weather in Seoul in October is bright and balmy.
All the hospital beds are full, and women with thick arms
and bent knees, feet in the stirrups, scream in an echoing
symphony. A woman with small ankles can't see
beyond her bloated stomach. She keeps her eyes shut
as forceps dig, doctors' hands twisting between her legs
like a corkscrew pulling out the plug.
It's been a busy morning, and between heaving breaths
she wonders *how much longer?* First the head,
then the shriveled body, bright as a small sun.
For the first time in her life she sighs and means it.
That's how it happens in my fantasy, the movie I watch
on repeat, re-imagined myth of my birth. No. I emerged
from seafoam flapping my tailfins in the Pacific froth.
I washed ashore encased in a mermaid purse, crawled on all fours,
and learned the power of breath. No. I was stardust,
an accumulation of space matter falling to earth in tiny pieces.
I'm still gathering my limbs. They're scattered all over the planet.
None of that is true. I was born in the airport, propelled
through the gaping mouth of sliding glass doors.
My father's second cousin ferried me down the stairs,
my mouth bubbling with Korean consonants, eyes still wary
of sight. In the video recording of my arrival, the airport light
burns everything so yellow it's purple. My grandfather's cheeks
behind his glasses glow like round speckled eggs. I've watched
the video so many times it's etched like a scar. I can feel
my mother's yellow tears fall purple on my cheek. My father
tucks his upper lip inside his tongue. Years later, I will learn
why he does this: searching for words when the mouth is lacking,

soft tears cradled in the pockets of his open eyes. What's the difference between memory told and memory burned? I was born in the womb of a stranger, my face a reflection of somebody else's shadow. If I told you that I missed you, would you believe me? Would I?

"/'məTHər/," "/'mīgrənt/," "/mun/," and "/'məŋki/" incorporate text from the Oxford English Dictionary entries on "mother," "migrant," "moon," and "monkey."

Harry Harlow was an American psychologist known for his experiments on the impact of maternal deprivation and contact comfort on children's psychological, social, and emotional development. He was one of the first psychologists to explore the "science" of love, and one of his most famous and controversial experiments included separating newborn rhesus monkeys from their mothers and providing them with various inanimate surrogates. Though these studies provided us with important insight into the relationship between caregivers and children, his experiments are believed to have been, in part, the motivation for the creation of laws for the ethical treatment of laboratory animals. The poem "Abstract" (page 37) borrows language from Harlow's research paper, "The Nature of Love."

"The Stolen Generation" features an erasure of the Aboriginal Protection Act of 1869 and the Aborigines Protection Act of 1886. It also uses a quote from the article, "Stolen generation payout" published by *The Age* on August 2, 2007.

"The Last Straw" borrows language from the article "US woman put adopted Russian son on one-way flight alone back to homeland" published by the *NY Post* on April 9, 2010. The article tells the story of Artyom Savelyev, who was adopted from Russia and subsequently relinquished when he was seven years old. This case was considered "the last straw" in a series of tragedies related to Russian/US adoptions and resulted in a temporary freeze on Russian adoptions to the United States.

"'Lost' first languages leave permanent mark on the brain, new study reveals" is the title of an article that appeared in *The Guardian* on November 20, 2014.

ACKNOWLEDGEMENTS

I am grateful to the editors of the following publications in which these poems, in some form, first appeared:

The Collagist: "The Night I Dreamed of Water"
Antenna::Signals: "Moon Yeong Shin" and "Child's Pre-Flight Report"
TENDE RLOIN: *"Where are you really from?"* and "Abstract" (p. 35 and p. 39)
The Spirit of the Staircase chapbook published by Antenna :: Press Street Press: *"Where are you really from?"* and "Abstract" (p. 35 and p. 39)
Apogee: "Revisionist History"
Hyphen Magazine: "'Lost' first languages leave permanent mark on the brain, new study reveals"
Texas Review: *"What orchard are you from?"* and "Petals"
The New Republic: "/ˈmīgrənt/"
The Indianapolis Review: "Mother of Rock" and "Mother of Cloth"
Guernica: "/ˈməTHər/"
Kweli Journal: "Operation Babylift"
Georgia Review: "Underwater Falsetto"
SWWIM: *"Did you know"*
Plume: "St. Rose of Lima"
Pleaides: "To Whom It May Concern:"
Poetry Northwest: "Harlow's Monkey"

I wouldn't be the writer I am today without Kundiman, a community that has bolstered, fed, and soothed me over and over throughout the years. I'm especially grateful to Kundiman's co-founders, Sarah

Gambito and Joseph Legaspi, for creating a space that filled a hole in my heart I didn't know I had.

A bouquet of gratitude for my teachers and mentors, who believed in my work even when I didn't and who modeled for me what it means to be a poet: Gabrielle Calvocoressi, Jennifer Chang, Suzanne Gardinier, Cathy Park Hong, A. Van Jordan, Jeffrey McDaniel, and Heather McHugh. Additional blossoms of appreciation for Debra Allbery, Director of the MFA Program at Warren Wilson College, whose opening lecture at my first residency inspired the title of this collection, and Paul Otremba, who taught me the careful art of putting a book together and whose spirit lives on in these pages. You're deeply missed.

I'm so grateful for friends who provided inspiration and vital feedback as I pushed these poems forward: Tamiko Beyer, Cathy Linh Che, Dan Lau, Muriel Leung, Leigh Lucas, Tariq Luthun, Trish Marshall, Soham Patel, and Nomi Stone. Special thanks to Marci Calabretta Cancio-Bello for her support in the ordering of this manuscript; your poetic sensibilities and attention to detail are impressive and hugely appreciated!

Thank you to Hub City Press for taking a chance on my book, especially Kate McMullen for her amazing work on the design and my brilliant editor, Leslie Sainz. Thank you both for your collaboration and for helping me bring this vision to life.

I owe a debt of gratitude to the Rona Jaffe Foundation whose financial support made my first trip back to Korea possible, and to JaeRan Kim, whose blog, "Harlow's Monkey: An Unapologetic Look at Transracial and Transnational Adoption," introduced me to the psychologist Harry Harlow and his research. Discovering this blog set me on a path to understand the relationship between adoption and attachment theory and sparked the writing of many of the poems that appear in this book. Additional thanks to Deborah Blum, author of *Love at Goon Park: Harry Harlow and the Science of Affection*, an informative biography on Harlow that helped me understand the man behind the experiments.

Hat tips to Nay Saysourinho, who introduced me to Eden Some's artwork; Eden Some for granting us permission to use his beautiful ink wash painting for the cover; and Rowan Ricardo Phillips who, during a workshop at Warren Wilson, suggested I re-visit William Blake's "Infant Sorrow," which enabled me to find the perfect epigraph to open this collection.

Thank you to my family for loving me and teaching me the joy of reading. Thank you for supporting my curiosity and creativity and for never denying me books and my favorite felt tip pens.

In *Beloved*, Toni Morrison writes, "She is a friend of mine. She gather me, man. The pieces I am, she gather them and give them back to me in all the right order." To all the beloved people who have gathered me and held me close over the years: my New Orleans community, SLC & Joshua Tree fam, the funky coterie, krewe of wingnuts, fellow wallies, KID smART birds, Argentina squad, teacher comrades, and especially Nikita, my sister-star, Stephanie, my chosen family, and Ross, my love—thank you for the joy and the laughter.

When I started writing these poems, I felt very alone in my journey as an Asian American adoptee writer. Since then, I've met some wonderful people who shared an understanding of the adoptee experience and a passion for poetry. Their friendship, care, insight, and compassion have meant the world to me. To my adoptee poet sisters, Sarah Audsley, Marci Calabretta Cancio-Bello, Ansley Moon, and Leah Silvieus: this book is for you.

Tiana Nobile is a Korean American adoptee, Kundiman fellow, and recipient of a Rona Jaffe Foundation Writer's Award. A finalist of the National Poetry Series and Kundiman Poetry Prize, she is the author of the chapbook, *The Spirit of the Staircase* (2017). Her writing has appeared in *Poetry Northwest, The New Republic, Guernica,* and the *Texas Review,* among others. Tiana received her BA from Sarah Lawrence College, MAT in Elementary and Special Education from the University of New Orleans, and MFA in Poetry from Warren Wilson College. She lives in New Orleans, Louisiana. For more, visit www.tiananobile.com.

PUBLISHING
New & Extraordinary
VOICES FROM THE
AMERICAN SOUTH

Founded in Spartanburg, South Carolina in 1995, Hub City Press has emerged as the South's premier independent literary press. Focused on finding and spotlighting extraordinary new and unsung writers from the American South, our curated list champions diverse authors and books that don't fit into the commercial publishing landscape. The press has published over ninety high-caliber literary works, including novels, short stories, poetry, memoir, and books emphasizing the region's culture and history. Hub City is interested in books with a strong sense of place and is committed to introducing a roster of lesser-heard Southern voices.

RECENT HUB CITY PRESS POETRY

Mustard, Milk, and Gin • Megan Denton Ray

Dusk & Dust • Esteban Rodriguez

Rodeo in Reverse • Lindsey Alexander

Eureka Mill - 20th Anniversary Edition • Ron Rash

Magic City Gospel • Ashley M. Jones

Wedding Pulls • J.K. Daniels

Punch • Ray McManus

Pantry • Lilah Hegnauer

Voodoo For the Other Woman • Angela Kelly

Waking • Ron Rash

Arno Pro Regular
10.5 / 14